# DIABETES DINING DISCOVERY

## A Flavorful Journey to Balanced Living and Better Health

**James B. Harris**

# Table of Contents

# Introduction

## Understanding Diabetes

Diabetes is a constant condition that influences how your body utilizes glucose (sugar). There are two primary sorts: type 1, where the body doesn't deliver insulin, and type 2, where the body doesn't utilize insulin appropriately. Overseeing diabetes includes observing glucose levels, a decent eating routine, normal activity, and a here-and-there prescription. It's significant to work intimately with medical services experts for customized care.

In type 1 diabetes, the resistant framework erroneously assaults and obliterates insulin-creating cells in the pancreas. This requires everyday insulin infusions. Type 2 diabetes is frequently created because of the way of life variables, hereditary qualities, or a mix. Way of life changes, for example, keeping a sound weight and being genuinely dynamic, assume a huge part in overseeing type 2 diabetes. Confusions can emerge while perhaps not very much made due, to influencing organs like the heart, kidneys, eyes, and nerves. Customary check-ups, glucose observation, and adherence to treatment plans are crucial for a successful diabetes board.

Confusions of diabetes incorporate cardiovascular issues, kidney sickness, nerve harm, and vision issues. High glucose levels over the long haul can prompt these entanglements. Observing blood glucose levels, taking recommended drugs, and embracing a sound way of life is urgent for counteraction. It's critical to know about side effects like over-the-top thirst, regular pee, and weariness, which might show uncontrolled diabetes. Early location and proactive administration essentially work on the personal satisfaction of people with diabetes. Ordinary clinical subsequent meet-ups assist with following advancement and changing treatment plans depending on the situation.

Diabetes the board includes keeping up with glucose inside target ranges through a blend of insulin or different drugs, diet, and exercise. Starch counting and glycemic list mindfulness are normal dietary methodologies. Customary actual work helps control weight and further develops insulin awareness. Constant glucose observing gadgets give continuous information, supporting better administration. Close-to-home prosperity is likewise critical, as stress can influence glucose levels. Diabetes schooling and care groups are significant assets for people and their families. By and large, an all-encompassing methodology that addresses physical, profound, and way of life factors is fundamental for powerful diabetes care.

# Importance of a Diabetes Meal Plan

A diabetes dinner plan is pivotal for overseeing glucose levels. It manages sugar consumption, controls segment estimates, and keeps a reasonable eating routine, supporting general well-being and forestalling intricacies related to diabetes.

Furthermore, a diabetes feast plan advances weight the board, brings down the gamble of cardiovascular issues, and upgrades energy levels. Predictable adherence to the arrangement engages people with diabetes to settle on informed food decisions and keep up with stable blood glucose levels over the day.

Moreover, a very much-planned diabetes feast plan can further develop insulin responsiveness, supporting better glucose control. It offers an organized way to deal with sustenance, consolidating various supplement thick food varieties that add to long-haul prosperity and may diminish the requirement for medicine changes.

Besides, a diabetes dinner plan cultivates familiarity with dietary propensities, empowering people to settle on better decisions. It assumes a critical part in forestalling complexities, for example, nerve harm, kidney issues, and vision issues, in this manner adding to a, generally speaking, a better life for those overseeing diabetes.

Likewise, a diabetes feast plan upholds glycemic control by disseminating dinners and snacks over the day, forestalling sharp vacillations in glucose levels. This solidness is fundamental for forestalling hyperglycemia or hypoglycemia, at last decreasing the gamble of intense difficulties and advancing supported well-being for people with diabetes.

# Chapter 1: Basics of Diabetes Nutrition

## Carbohydrates, Proteins, and Fats

For diabetes the board, it's urgent to screen starch admission to control glucose levels. Pick complex carbs like entire grains and breaking point straightforward sugars. Protein settles glucose; select lean sources like poultry. Remember solid fats for control, like those from avocados and nuts. Consistency in segment sizes and dinner timing is key for diabetic nourishment. Continuously counsel medical services proficient for customized exhortation.

In diabetes the board, understanding the glycemic file (GI) can be helpful. Food varieties with a lower GI discharge glucose all the more leisurely, directing glucose. Fiber-rich food sources help in assimilation and can likewise assist with controlling glucose levels. Customary actual work supplements a reasonable eating routine for generally speaking diabetes care. Observing and adjusting your eating regimen in light of individual reactions and counseling a medical care group are critical parts of compelling diabetes the board.

While overseeing diabetes, focusing on segment control is fundamental. Eating more modest, adjusted feasts for the day can assist with forestalling glucose spikes. Remain hydrated, pick food varieties with a blend of supplements, and be aware of liquor consumption. Ordinary glucose checking gives important criticism on how your body answers various food sources and exercises. Customized changes in your way of life, under the direction of medical services experts, add to successful diabetes care.

Also, it's vital to know about secret sugars in handled food varieties and refreshments. Perusing names can assist with recognizing wellsprings of added sugars. By building an emotionally supportive network and remaining informed about diabetes the board methodologies can add to long-haul achievement. Keep in mind that a comprehensive methodology that consolidates sustenance, actual work, and customary clinical check-ups is critical to overseeing diabetes.

Trying different things with dinner timing and separating can likewise be useful. Certain individuals with diabetes make progress with more modest, more incessant feasts, while others lean toward a couple of bigger dinners. Observing glucose levels when feasts can direct these changes. Stress the board and sufficient rest assume parts in general prosperity, affecting glucose control. Consistency and open correspondence with medical care experts stay urgent in refining your customized diabetes-the-board plan.

Consistently checking and understanding your Hemoglobin A1c levels gives a more extensive perspective on your glucose command over the long run. It's an important instrument for evaluating the viability of your diabetes board plan. Feel free to direct an enlisted dietitian, diabetes teacher, or other medical services experts to tweak your dietary decisions and way of life for ideal diabetes care. Keep in mind that little economic changes can prompt huge upgrades by and large the well-being and diabetes of the executives.

# Glycemic Index and Load

The glycemic file (GI) measures how rapidly a sugar-containing food raises blood glucose levels. High-GI food sources might cause fast spikes, while low-GI food sources lead to slower, more progressive increments. The glycemic load (GL) considers both the GI and how much sugars are consumed, giving a more far-reaching view. For diabetes the executives, zeroing in on lower-GI and moderate-GL food sources can assist with keeping up with stable glucose levels. Models incorporate entire grains, vegetables, and non-bland vegetables. It's fundamental to offset carbs with different supplements and talk with medical services proficient for customized guidance.

To expand further, people with diabetes frequently benefit from picking carbs with a lower influence on glucose. Low-GI food varieties, like yams, quinoa, and beans, are processed all the more leisurely, forestalling quick spikes in glucose. Overseeing glycemic load includes choosing low-GI food sources as well as being aware of part estimates.

Counting fiber-rich food varieties can likewise be gainful, as fiber dials back the processing and retention of carbs, adding to more steady glucose levels. Moreover, matching starches with protein and solid fats can additionally assist with managing blood glucose.

Normal checking of glucose, alongside a decent eating routine, standard active work, and prescription as recommended, are key parts of viable diabetes on the board. Continuously talk with medical care experts for customized direction given individual well-being needs.

While considering diabetes the executives, focusing on the general nature of your diet is fundamental. Pick entire, natural food sources, and breaking point for the admission of refined carbs and sugars. Picking different brilliant vegetables, lean proteins, and sound fats upholds a balanced and nutritious eating routine.

Segment control plays a pivotal part. Eating more modest, adjusted dinners for the day can assist with controlling glucose levels. It's additionally valuable to be aware of the planning of feasts, dividing them equitably to keep away from delayed periods without food.

Standard actual work is a strong supplement to dietary decisions. Practice improves insulin awareness and can add to all the more likely glucose control. Talk with medical care experts to tailor a diabetes-the-board plan that lines up with your particular necessities and well-being objectives.

Close to dietary contemplations, remaining hydrated is significant for diabetes executives. Water controls glucose levels and supports by and large well-being. Be wary of sweet beverages, as they can prompt quick spikes in blood glucose.

Checking glucose levels consistently takes into account better comprehension of what various food sources and way of life factors mean for individual reactions. This data enables people to settle on informed decisions and change their methodology depending on the situation.

Moreover, stress the executives and adequate rest are basic pieces of diabetes care. Constant pressure and deficient rest can influence glucose levels and in general prosperity. Laying out a steady rest routine and integrating pressure-diminishing exercises, like care or actual activity, can decidedly impact diabetes the executives.

Keep in mind, that individual reactions to food and way of life elements can change, so it's vital to work intimately with medical care experts for customized direction and backing.

With regards to carbs, picking those with a lower influence on glucose is urgent. Entire grains like earthy-colored rice, quinoa, and oats, as well as vegetables like lentils and chickpeas, are incredible decisions.

With regards to fats, focus on solid fats like those tracked down in avocados, nuts, seeds, and olive oil. These fats can assist with satiety and add to general heart well-being.

Customary glucose checking assists you with understanding how your body answers various food sources. This knowledge considers powerful changes in your eating regimen and way of life decisions. Working cooperatively with medical care suppliers guarantees a thorough and customized way to deal with diabetes executives.

Ultimately, keeping an emotionally supportive network and remaining informed about the most recent improvements in diabetes care can add to a comprehensive and proactive way to deal with dealing with the condition.

It's vital to know about secret sugars in handled food varieties. Perusing food marks can assist with recognizing wellsprings of added sugars, which can affect glucose levels. Picking entire, natural food varieties and planning feasts at home gives better command over fixings.

Ordinary activity is a useful asset in diabetes the board. Both high-impact works, such as strolling or cycling, and strength preparation can add to further developed insulin responsiveness and generally speaking prosperity.

For those with diabetes, remaining informed about new exploration, drugs, and treatment choices is important. Constant learning guarantees that people can settle on informed conclusions about their consideration and exploit progressions in diabetes the board.

Keep in mind that overseeing diabetes is a long-lasting excursion, and progressing correspondence with medical services experts is critical to adjusting procedures and keeping up with ideal well-being.

# Portion Control

For diabetes executives, rehearsing segment control is essential. Center around offset feasts with controlled carb admission to assist with managing glucose levels. Consider counseling a medical care proficient or a nutritionist for customized exhortation.

Pick entire grains, lean proteins, and a lot of vegetables. Use estimating apparatuses to check partitions, and be aware of added sugars and soaked fats. Little, successive feasts can assist with settling glucose over the day. Ordinary activity supplements a sound eating routine for better diabetes the board.

Moreover, pick food sources with a low glycemic record, as they slowly affect glucose. Consolidate sound fats, like those from avocados and nuts. Remain hydrated and screen your glucose levels routinely to comprehend what various food sources mean for you. Consistency in your dietary patterns and way of life is key to overseeing diabetes successfully.

Explore different avenues regarding feast timing; certain individuals benefit from uniformly separated dinners, while others make progress with irregular fasting. Be wary of liquor, as it can influence glucose levels. Keep in mind, that individual reactions to food change, so focus on how your body responds and change your eating regimen likewise. Normal check-ups with medical care experts can assist with refining your diabetes executive plan because of your exceptional requirements.

Consider counseling an enrolled dietitian who has practical experience in diabetes care for customized direction. Keep a food diary to follow your feasts, partitions, and glucose levels. Pick cooking techniques like barbecuing, steaming, or baking as opposed to broiling. Building an emotionally supportive network can likewise help keep a sound way of life and oversee diabetes successfully.

Focus on fiber-rich food varieties like natural products, vegetables, and entire grains, as they can assist with settling glucose levels. Be aware of stowed-away sugars in handled food varieties and drinks. Investigate elective sugars, yet use them with some restraint. Keep in mind, that little, steady changes in your dietary patterns are more reasonable and can prompt long-haul progress in overseeing diabetes.

Routinely screen your part measures by utilizing more modest plates and bowls. Make a steady feast timetable to assist with managing glucose. Participate in careful eating, focusing on craving and totality signs. Hold back nothing adjusted diet that incorporates different supplements. Assuming you have explicit inquiries regarding food varieties or dinner arrangements, go ahead and request more custom-made guidance.

Incorporate a blend of bright vegetables to guarantee a different scope of supplements. Select lean protein sources like poultry, fish, and vegetables. Try not to skip feasts, and stay away from exorbitant nibbling. Remain instructed about the glycemic record of food varieties to pursue informed decisions. Keep in mind, that control and assortment are key parts of a decent eating routine for diabetes executives.

Explore different avenues regarding spices and flavors to add flavor without depending on inordinate salt or sugar. Practice careful eating by relishing each chomp and staying away from interruptions during dinners. Remain mindful of part creep, particularly during get-togethers. Consistently audit and change your dinner plan given your reaction to various food sources and any progressions in your wellbeing or way of life.

Integrate normal actual work into your daily practice, as it further develops insulin responsiveness. Go for the gold of high-impact activities and strength preparation. Remain informed about your drugs and counsel your medical care group before rolling out huge improvements to your eating routine or exercise plan. Consistency and progressing self-checking are key components in actually overseeing diabetes and advancing in general prosperity.

# Chapter 2: Building a Balanced Plate

## The Plate Method

The Plate Method is a helpful tool for managing diabetes by creating balanced meals. It involves dividing your plate into sections for different food groups: half for non-starchy vegetables, a quarter for lean protein, and a quarter for carbohydrates. This promotes balanced nutrition and helps control blood sugar levels. Remember to choose whole grains, control portion sizes, and consider including healthy fats for optimal balance.

When following the Plate Method for diabetes, focus on incorporating a variety of colorful vegetables to maximize nutrients. Opt for lean protein sources such as poultry, fish, tofu, or legumes. Choose complex carbohydrates like whole grains, brown rice, or quinoa, and be mindful of portion sizes to avoid overeating. Additionally, include sources of healthy fats like avocados or olive oil for added satiety. Regular monitoring of blood sugar levels and consulting with a healthcare professional can help tailor this approach to individual needs.

In addition to the Plate Method, consider spreading your meals and snacks throughout the day to help regulate blood sugar levels. Regular physical activity is crucial for diabetes management, as it enhances insulin sensitivity. Stay hydrated, choose foods with a low glycemic index, and be mindful of added sugars. Monitoring your blood sugar regularly will provide valuable insights into how different foods and lifestyle choices impact your levels. Collaborate with your healthcare team to fine-tune your approach to personalized diabetes management.

Experiment with incorporating a variety of herbs and spices into your meals to enhance flavor without relying on excessive salt or sugar. Fiber-rich foods, like fruits, vegetables, and whole grains, can contribute to better blood sugar control and improved digestive health. Remember that individual responses to foods can vary, so pay attention to how your body reacts to different meals. A food diary may help identify patterns and make adjustments to your diabetes management plan. Lastly, prioritize stress management and adequate sleep, as they also play roles in overall well-being and blood sugar regulation.

When dining out or preparing meals, educate yourself about food choices and portion sizes. Opt for grilled, baked, or steamed dishes instead of fried options. Restaurants often provide nutritional information, helping you make informed decisions. Don't forget the importance of regular check-ups with your healthcare team for ongoing support and adjustments to your diabetes management plan.

Being proactive and knowledgeable empowers you to make healthier choices, contributing to long-term well-being

The Plate Method is a helpful tool for managing diabetes by creating balanced meals. It involves dividing your plate into sections for different food groups: half for non-starchy vegetables, a quarter for lean protein, and a quarter for carbohydrates. This promotes balanced nutrition and helps control blood sugar levels. Remember to choose whole grains, control portion sizes, and consider including healthy fats for optimal balance.

When following the Plate Method for diabetes, focus on incorporating a variety of colorful vegetables to maximize nutrients. Opt for lean protein sources such as poultry, fish, tofu, or legumes. Choose complex carbohydrates like whole grains, brown rice, or quinoa, and be mindful of portion sizes to avoid overeating. Additionally, include sources of healthy fats like avocados or olive oil for added satiety. Regular monitoring of blood sugar levels and consulting with a healthcare professional can help tailor this approach to individual needs.

In addition to the Plate Method, consider spreading your meals and snacks throughout the day to help regulate blood sugar levels. Regular physical activity is crucial for diabetes management, as it enhances insulin sensitivity. Stay hydrated, choose foods with a low glycemic index, and be mindful of added sugars. Monitoring your blood sugar regularly will provide valuable insights into how different foods and lifestyle choices impact your levels. Collaborate with your healthcare team to fine-tune your approach to personalized diabetes management.

Experiment with incorporating a variety of herbs and spices into your meals to enhance flavor without relying on excessive salt or sugar. Fiber-rich foods, like fruits, vegetables, and whole grains, can contribute to better blood sugar control and improved digestive health. Remember that individual responses to foods can vary, so pay attention to how your body reacts to different meals. A food diary may help identify patterns and make adjustments to your diabetes management plan. Lastly, prioritize stress management and adequate sleep, as they also play roles in overall well-being and blood sugar regulation.

More

ChatGPT

When dining out or preparing meals, educate yourself about food choices and portion sizes. Opt for grilled, baked, or steamed dishes instead of fried options. Restaurants often provide nutritional information, helping you make informed decisions. Don't forget the importance of regular check-ups with your healthcare team for ongoing support and adjustments to your diabetes management plan. Being proactive and knowledgeable empowers you to make healthier choices, contributing to long-term well-being

# Smart Food Choices

For a reasonable plate with diabetes, center around lean proteins like chicken or fish, non-bland vegetables, and entire grains. Limit refined carbs, choose sound fats, and control segment sizes to oversee glucose levels successfully.

Incorporate fiber-rich food varieties like beans, lentils, and vegetables to assist with balancing out glucose. Pick entire natural products over natural product squeezes, and integrate sound bites like nuts or Greek yogurt. Remain hydrated and consider counseling a nutritionist for customized guidance.

Focus on low-glycemic file food sources, for example, quinoa and yams. Screen starch admission, dispersing it uniformly over the day. Decide on cooking techniques like barbecuing, steaming, or baking as opposed to broiling. Customary active work supplements a decent eating regimen for better diabetes executives.

Explore different avenues regarding spices and flavors for flavor without added sugars or salt. Screen glucose levels consistently and change your eating regimen in like manner. Pick unsweetened drinks, and be aware of stowed-away sugars in bundled food varieties. Team up with a medical care professional to tailor an arrangement that suits your particular requirements and way of life.

Consider remembering greasy fish rich in omega-3s, similar to salmon, for heart wellbeing. Oversee pressure, as it can influence glucose levels. Try not to skip dinners, and plan steady eating times. Know about liquor utilization and its possible impacts on glucose. Routinely survey your feast plan with medical services suppliers for progressing support.

Investigate low-calorie, supplement thick snacks like crude vegetables with hummus. Go for the gold assortment of vegetables to guarantee a wide scope of supplements. Try different things with various cooking oils like olive oil for better fats. Recall that singular reactions to food varieties change, so track how your body responds to various dinners.

Integrate care into dietary patterns, appreciating each chomp and focusing on craving and completion signs. Choose entire grains like earthy-colored rice and entire wheat pasta for supported energy. Be wary of handled food varieties, as they might contain stowed-away sugars and unfortunate fats. Routinely teach yourself about diabetes the board and sustenance refreshes for informed decisions.

Consider counseling an enlisted dietitian to make a customized feast plan custom-made to your diabetes board objectives. Investigate elective sugars with some restraint, and pick snacks with an equilibrium between protein and fiber. Remember the significance of a decent night's rest, as it adds to general prosperity and can influence glucose guidelines. Consistently survey and change your feast plan in light of your body's reaction and any progressions in your well-being.

Take part in proactive tasks you appreciate, as standard activity can further develop insulin responsiveness. Keep solid snacks promptly accessible to try not to settle on incautious food decisions. Explore different avenues regarding different cooking strategies to upgrade the kinds of your dinners without compromising dietary benefits. Remain all around hydrated, as water is fundamental for different physical processes and can help with overseeing glucose levels. Continuously discuss transparently with your medical services group about any progressions or difficulties you experience in your diabetes the board venture.

# Chapter 3: Breakfast Ideas

## Low-Glycemic Breakfasts

Consider choices like steel-cut cereal, Greek yogurt with berries, or eggs with vegetables for a low-glycemic breakfast that can assist with overseeing glucose levels in diabetes.

You could likewise partake in a morning meal of entire grain toast with avocado, a smoothie with salad greens and low-glycemic natural products, or a chia seed pudding with unsweetened almond milk. These decisions give supported energy without causing fast spikes in glucose.

you could attempt a morning meal bowl with quinoa, nuts, and seeds, or curds with cut cucumbers and cherry tomatoes. Another choice is a veggie omelet or a frittata made with spinach, mushrooms, and tomatoes. These dinners offer a decent equilibrium between supplements and assist with keeping up with stable glucose levels.

Think about a morning meal parfait with layers of Greek yogurt, nuts, and berries, or an entire grain wrap with lean protein like turkey or chicken, alongside veggies. Furthermore, almond spread on entire grain toast or a serving of smoked salmon with entire grain wafers can be fulfilling and low-glycemic.

What about attempting a morning meal salad with blended greens, cherry tomatoes, and barbecued chicken, or a sans sugar, entire grain cereal with unsweetened almond milk? These choices can be scrumptious and give various supplements while holding the glycemic influence under tight restraints.

You could partake in a green smoothie with salad greens, cucumber, and a little piece of low-glycemic organic products like berries. Another thought is a morning meal quinoa bowl with diced apples, cinnamon, and a sprinkle of nuts for added crunch. These choices are diabetes-accommodating as well as delectable and nutritious.

# Balanced Smoothies

For a reasonable smoothie appropriate for somebody with diabetes, have a go at joining spinach, berries, unsweetened almond milk, and a limited quantity of Greek yogurt. This gives fiber, cell reinforcements, and protein without unnecessary sugar.

Another diabetes-accommodating smoothie choice is to mix avocado, cucumber, and a modest bunch of kale, and add unsweetened coconut water. This blend offers solid fats, fiber, and an insignificant effect on glucose levels. Make sure to screen segment sizes and individual reactions to fixings.

What about a smoothie with a base of chia seeds absorbed water, blended in with a moderate measure of strawberries, a sprinkle of unsweetened soy milk, and a dash of cinnamon? This gives omega-3 unsaturated fats, fiber, and a sprinkle of pleasantness without added sugars. Change fixing amounts in light of individual inclinations and dietary requirements.

Here is an itemized rundown of elements for a diabetes-accommodating smoothie:

Green Smoothie:

Spinach or kale

Berries (e.g., blueberries, raspberries)

Unsweetened almond milk

Greek yogurt (unsweetened)

Ice blocks (discretionary)

Avocado and Greens Smoothie:

Avocado

Cucumber

Kale or spinach

Unsweetened coconut water

Ice blocks (discretionary)

Chia Seed and Strawberry Smoothie:

Chia seeds (absorbed water)

Strawberries

Unsweetened soy milk

Cinnamon

Ice blocks (discretionary)

Make sure to change fixing amounts because of taste inclinations and dietary necessities.

Here is another diabetes-accommodating smoothie choice:

Berry Almond Protein Smoothie:

Blended berries (e.g., raspberries, strawberries)

Unsweetened almond milk

Whey protein powder (low sugar)

Almond margarine (unsweetened)

Ice blocks (discretionary)

Mix these elements for a smoothie that joins the cell reinforcement force of berries with the protein and sound fats from almond margarine and almond milk. Change the amounts because of your inclinations and wholesome necessities.

# Chapter 4: Lunch and Dinner Recipes

## Lean Protein Options

Diabetes patients can pick lean protein sources like skinless poultry, fish, tofu, beans, and vegetables to assist with overseeing glucose levels successfully.

Here are some diabetes-accommodating fixings:

Lean Proteins:

Chicken bosom

Turkey

Fish (salmon, fish)

Tofu

Lentils

Non-Dull Vegetables:

Spinach

Broccoli

Cauliflower

Ringer peppers

Zucchini

Entire Grains:

Quinoa

Earthy colored rice

Oats

Grain

Solid Fats:

Olive oil

Avocado

Nuts (almonds, pecans)

Low-Fat Dairy:

Greek yogurt

Skim milk

Curds

Spices and Flavors:

Garlic

Ginger

Cinnamon

Turmeric

Organic products (with some restraint):

Berries (strawberries, blueberries)

Apples

Pears

Make sure to control segment measures and talk with a medical service proficient or an enlisted dietitian for customized guidance.

Here is a basic and diabetes-accommodating recipe for Barbecued Lemon Spice Chicken with Quinoa:

Barbecued Lemon Spice Chicken with Quinoa:

Fixings:

4 boneless, skinless chicken bosoms

2 lemons (squeezed and zested)

2 tablespoons olive oil

2 cloves garlic (minced)

1 teaspoon dried oregano

1 teaspoon dried thyme

Salt and pepper to taste

1 cup quinoa

2 cups low-sodium chicken stock

New parsley (slashed for embellish)

Directions:

Marinate the Chicken:

In a bowl, combine lemon juice, lemon zing, olive oil, minced garlic, oregano, thyme, salt, and pepper.

Place chicken bosoms in a Ziploc pack and pour half of the marinade over them. Seal the pack and allow it to marinate in the fridge for no less than 30 minutes.

Preheat the Barbecue:

Preheat your barbecue to medium-high intensity.

Barbecue the Chicken:

Eliminate chicken from the marinade and dispose of the pre-owned marinade. Barbecue the chicken for around 6-8 minutes for every side or until completely cooked.

Plan Quinoa:

While the chicken is barbecuing, flush quinoa under chilly water. In a pot, consolidate quinoa and chicken stock. Heat to the point of boiling, then decrease intensity, cover, and stew for 15 minutes or until quinoa is cooked.

Serve:

Plate the barbecued chicken over a bed of cooked quinoa.

Shower the leftover marinade over the chicken.

Embellish with hacked new parsley.

Partake in your tasty and adjusted dinner! Change segments in light of individual dietary requirements.

Here is a recipe for a tasty and diabetes-accommodating Vegetable Pan fried food with Tofu:

Vegetable Sautéed food with Tofu:

Fixings:

1 block extra-firm tofu, squeezed and cubed

2 tablespoons low-sodium soy sauce

1 tablespoon sesame oil

1 tablespoon olive oil

2 cloves garlic, minced

1 tablespoon ginger, ground

1 cup broccoli florets

1 ringer pepper, meagerly cut

1 carrot, julienned

1 cup snap peas

1 cup mushrooms, cut

2 green onions, slashed

1 tablespoon rice vinegar

1 teaspoon honey or a sugar substitute

Sesame seeds for decorating

Cooked earthy-colored rice for serving

Guidelines:

Plan Tofu:

Press tofu to eliminate the abundance of water and cut it into blocks.

In a bowl, blend cubed tofu with soy sauce and allow it to marinate for 15-20 minutes.

Cook Tofu:

Heat olive oil in a huge skillet over medium intensity.

Add marinated tofu and cook until brilliant brown on all sides. Put away.

Pan sear Vegetables:

In a similar skillet, add sesame oil, garlic, and ginger. Sauté briefly.

Add broccoli, ringer pepper, carrot, snap peas, and mushrooms. Pan-sear until vegetables are delicate and fresh.

Join Tofu and Vegetables:

Return cooked tofu to the skillet and throw to join with the vegetables.

Plan Sauce:

In a little bowl, blend soy sauce, rice vinegar, and honey. Pour the sauce over the tofu and vegetable combination. Mix well to cover.

Serve:

Serve the sautéed food over prepared earthy-colored rice.

Decorate with cleaved green onions and sesame seeds.

Partake in this scrumptious and nutritious Vegetable Pan fried food with Tofu as a fantastic dinner! Change the fixings given your inclinations and dietary requirements.

# Healthy Carbohydrates

Entire grains like earthy-colored rice, quinoa, and oats, alongside vegetables and vegetables, are great wellsprings of sound carbs for diabetes patients. These choices give fiber and fundamental supplements while overseeing glucose levels.

Also, organic products like berries, apples, and pears are phenomenal decisions because of their fiber content. Yams and beans are other nutritious choices that discharge glucose slowly, advancing better glucose control for people with diabetes.

For a diabetes-accommodating dinner, consider consolidating fixings, for example,

Entire grains: Earthy colored rice, quinoa, entire wheat, oats.

Vegetables: Salad greens, broccoli, cauliflower, ringer peppers.

Vegetables: Lentils, chickpeas, dark beans.

Organic products: Berries, apples, pears, citrus organic products.

Lean Proteins: Chicken, turkey, fish, tofu, vegetables.

Solid Fats: Avocado, olive oil, nuts, seeds.

Dairy or Dairy Choices: Low-fat yogurt, almond milk, or other low-fat choices.

These fixings can be consolidated inventively to plan adjusted and fulfilling dinners for those overseeing diabetes.

here is a basic and diabetes-accommodating recipe for a Quinoa and Vegetable Sautéed food:

Fixings:

1 cup quinoa (flushed)

2 cups blended vegetables (broccoli, ringer peppers, carrots)

1 cup diced tofu or cooked chicken bosom

2 cloves garlic (minced)

1 tablespoon low-sodium soy sauce

1 tablespoon olive oil

1 teaspoon ginger (ground)

Salt and pepper to taste

Slashed green onions to decorate

Guidelines:

Cook quinoa as indicated by bundle guidelines.

In an enormous skillet, heat olive oil over medium intensity. Add garlic and ginger, and sauté until fragrant.

Add blended vegetables and cook until marginally delicate.

Mix in tofu or chicken, and cook until protein is warmed through.

Add cooked quinoa to the skillet, sprinkle soy sauce over the blend, and throw everything together.

Season with salt and pepper to taste.

Embellish with cleaved green onions before serving.

This recipe consolidates protein, solid carbs, and veggies for a fair feast reasonable for those with diabetes. Change fixings to your inclinations and dietary requirements.

Here is a diabetes-accommodating recipe for Prepared Salmon with Simmered Vegetables:

Fixings:

4 salmon filets

2 cups broccoli florets

1 cup cherry tomatoes, split

1 cup child carrots, split longwise

2 tablespoons olive oil

2 cloves garlic, minced

1 teaspoon dried oregano

1 teaspoon lemon zing

Salt and pepper to taste

New lemon wedges for serving

Directions:

Preheat the stove to 400°F (200°C).

Put salmon filets on a baking sheet fixed with material paper.

In a bowl, throw broccoli, cherry tomatoes, and carrots with olive oil, garlic, oregano, lemon zing, salt, and pepper.

Spread the vegetable blend around the salmon filets on the baking sheet.

Heat in the preheated broiler for 15-20 minutes or until the salmon is cooked through and drops effectively with a fork.

Serve the heated salmon over a bed of simmered vegetables, and topping with new lemon wedges.

This recipe gives a sound portion of omega-3 unsaturated fats from the salmon and various brilliant vegetables, making it a nutritious and flavorful choice for those with diabetes.

Here is a diabetes-accommodating recipe for a Quinoa Salad with Chickpeas and Mediterranean Flavors:

Fixings:

1 cup quinoa, washed

1 can (15 oz) chickpeas, depleted and washed

1 cup cherry tomatoes, split

1 cucumber, diced

1/2 cup Kalamata olives, cut

1/4 cup red onion, finely hacked

1/4 cup feta cheddar, disintegrated

2 tablespoons extra-virgin olive oil

1 tablespoon red wine vinegar

1 teaspoon dried oregano

Salt and pepper to taste

New parsley for embellish

Directions:

Cook quinoa as per bundle guidelines and let it cool.

In a huge bowl, join cooled quinoa, chickpeas, cherry tomatoes, cucumber, olives, red onion, and feta cheddar.

In a little bowl, whisk together olive oil, red wine vinegar, dried oregano, salt, and pepper.

Pour the dressing over the quinoa blend and throw to consolidate.

Embellish with new parsley before serving.

This invigorating quinoa salad is loaded with fiber, protein, and Mediterranean flavors, making it a delightful and diabetes-accommodating dinner.

# Fiber-rich Vegetables

Diabetes patients can profit from fiber-rich vegetables like broccoli, spinach, kale, cauliflower, and Brussels sprouts. These veggies assist with overseeing glucose levels and give fundamental supplements.

Incorporate fiber-stuffed vegetables like carrots, chime peppers, zucchini, and artichokes into your eating routine. They offer a decent equilibrium of supplements while advancing stable glucose levels for people with diabetes.

For a diabetes-accommodating feast, consider integrating fixings like lean proteins (chicken, fish), non-dull vegetables (mixed greens, broccoli), entire grains (quinoa, earthy-colored rice), and vegetables (lentils, beans). Utilize sound fats like olive oil and pick low-sugar flavors for some extra zing.

Attempt a basic diabetes-accommodating recipe:

Barbecued Lemon Spice Chicken with Quinoa and Simmered Vegetables:

Fixings:

Boneless, skinless chicken bosoms

Lemon juice

Olive oil

New spices (rosemary, thyme)

Garlic, minced

Salt and pepper

Quinoa

Grouped vegetables (zucchini, chime peppers, cherry tomatoes)

Guidelines:

Marinate chicken in a combination of lemon juice, olive oil, minced garlic, new spices, salt, and pepper.

Barbecue the chicken until completely cooked.

Cook quinoa as per bundle guidelines.

Throw arranged vegetables in olive oil, salt, and pepper, then cook until delicate.

Serve barbecued chicken on a bed of quinoa with cooked vegetables as an afterthought.

Make sure to talk with a medical care professional or a nutritionist for customized dietary counsel.

Absolutely! Here is another diabetes-accommodating recipe:

Salmon and Vegetable Pan fried food:

Fixings:

Salmon filets

Broccoli florets

Chime peppers (arranged colors)

Snow peas

Ginger, minced

Garlic, minced

Low-sodium soy sauce

Sesame oil

Earthy colored rice (discretionary)

Guidelines:

Cut salmon into reduced-down pieces.

Pan-sear salmon in a container with minced ginger and garlic until cooked.

Add broccoli, chime peppers, and snow peas to the container and sautéed food until vegetables are delicate and fresh.

Blend in low-sodium soy sauce and a sprinkle of sesame oil for some extra zing.

Serve over earthy-colored rice whenever wanted.

This recipe is rich in omega-3 unsaturated fats from salmon and incorporates brilliant vegetables for added supplements. Change segment sizes in light of individual dietary requirements.

# Chapter 5: Snack Options

## Nutritious Snacks

Settle snacks with an equilibrium of fiber, protein, and sound fats. Models incorporate crude veggies with hummus, Greek yogurt with berries, or a small bunch of nuts. Keep away from sweet choices and focus on entire, natural food varieties.

Consider choices like cut apple with peanut butter, hard-bubbled eggs, or cherry tomatoes with mozzarella. Nuts like almonds and pecans, as well as seeds, are amazing decisions. Moreover, settle on low-carb vegetables like cucumber or celery matched with a moderate measure of cheddar. Hold segments under control to oversee glucose levels.

For a nutritious tidbit, consider fixings like:

Crude Vegetables: Cucumber, celery, chime peppers, cherry tomatoes.

Natural products: Berries, apple cuts.

Proteins: Hummus, Greek yogurt, hard-bubbled eggs, peanut butter, cheddar.

Nuts and Seeds: Almonds, pecans, chia seeds.

Dairy: Mozzarella cheddar or low-fat cheddar choices.

Consolidate these fixings inventively to make fulfilling and diabetes-accommodating bites. Continuously be aware of part measures and talk with a medical care proficient for customized dietary exhortation.

Indeed, the following are several basic and nutritious nibble recipes for diabetes-accommodating choices:

Greek Yogurt Parfait:

Fixings:

1 cup Greek yogurt

1/2 cup blended berries (strawberries, blueberries, raspberries)

1 tablespoon chia seeds

1 tablespoon hacked nuts (almonds, pecans)

Directions:

In a bowl, layer Greek yogurt.

Add a layer of blended berries.

Sprinkle chia seeds and slashed nuts on top.

Rehash the layers.

Partake in a scrumptious and fulfilling parfait.

Veggie and Hummus Plate:

Fixings:

Grouped crude vegetables (carrot sticks, cucumber cuts, chime pepper strips)

1/4 cup hummus

Directions:

Orchestrate the crude vegetables on a plate.

Present with a side of hummus for plunging.

Partake in a crunchy and tasty nibble rich in fiber and supplements.

Make sure to adjust these recipes given individual inclinations and dietary necessities.

Absolutely! The following are a couple more diabetes-accommodating nibble thoughts:

Apple Peanut Butter Sandwiches:

Fixings:

Apple cuts (cored)

Regular peanut butter (no additional sugar)

Guidelines:

Spread peanut butter on one side of an apple cut.

Top with one more apple cut to make a "sandwich."

Rehash to make extra apple peanut butter sandwiches.

Partake in a sweet and fulfilling treat.

Nutty Seed Blend:

Fixings:

Almonds

Pecans

Pumpkin seeds

Sunflower seeds

Directions:

Blend equivalent pieces of almonds, pecans, pumpkin seeds, and sunflower seeds.

Segment out a little small bunch for a speedy and crunchy nibble.

This blend gives a decent equilibrium between sound fats and protein.

These recipes are basic, scrumptious, and intended to assist with overseeing glucose levels. Change segment sizes to fit individual dietary requirements.

# Managing Blood Sugar Between Meals

For overseeing glucose between dinners for diabetes patients, center around adjusted, low-glycemic snacks like nuts, veggies, or lean proteins. Screen segment sizes, remain hydrated, and consider ordinary, moderate activity to assist with managing glucose levels.

separating dinners uniformly over the day can assist with settling glucose. Pick entire grains over refined starches and incorporate fiber-rich food sources. Screen glucose consistently, and if taking drugs, follow the recommended dose. Focus on a steady and sound way of life to help in general glucose control.

Select an even eating routine with a blend of entire grains, lean proteins (like poultry, fish, and tofu), a lot of vegetables, and sound fats (like avocados or nuts). Remember food varieties rich in fiber, as it helps with glucose guidelines. Limit handled food varieties, sweet tidbits, and high-carb choices. Individual dietary necessities might change, so counsel medical services proficient or an enrolled dietitian for customized direction.

Integrate these diabetes-accommodating fixings into your dinners:

Entire Grains: Quinoa, earthy colored rice, oats.

Lean Proteins: Chicken, turkey, fish, tofu, beans, lentils.

Vegetables: Mixed greens, broccoli, cauliflower, ringer peppers.

Sound Fats: Avocado, olive oil, nuts, seeds.

Fiber-rich food sources: Berries, apples, beans, lentils, and entire grains.

Low-glycemic food sources: Yams, vegetables, non-bland vegetables.

Dairy or Choices: Low-fat or without-fat choices.

Spices and Flavors: Use spices and flavors for flavor without adding additional salt or sugar.

Keep in mind, that segment control is vital, and individual dietary requirements might differ. Changes ought to be made given individual well-being objectives and particular dietary suggestions from medical services experts.

Here is a straightforward and diabetes-accommodating recipe for Barbecued Chicken and Vegetable Quinoa Bowl:

Fixings:

1 cup quinoa, cooked

2 boneless, skinless chicken bosoms

2 cups blended vegetables (e.g., chime peppers, zucchini, cherry tomatoes)

2 tablespoons olive oil

1 teaspoon garlic powder

1 teaspoon paprika

Salt and pepper to taste

New lemon juice (discretionary)

Guidelines:

Preheat the barbecue or barbecue dish.

Season the chicken bosoms with garlic powder, paprika, salt, and pepper.

In a bowl, throw the blended vegetables in with olive oil, salt, and pepper.

Barbecue the chicken for around 6-7 minutes for each side or until cooked through.

During the most recent couple of minutes of barbecuing the chicken, add the vegetables to the barbecue and cook until they are delicate and somewhat burned.

While barbecuing, get ready quinoa as indicated by bundle guidelines.

Cut the barbecued chicken into strips.

Gather bowls by setting a piece of quinoa, barbecued chicken, and vegetables.

Sprinkle with new lemon juice whenever wanted.

Make sure to change segment sizes in light of individual dietary necessities and talk with medical care experts for customized exhortation.

Here is a diabetes-accommodating recipe for a Salmon and Asparagus Foil Parcel:

Fixings:

2 salmon filets

1 pack of asparagus, managed

1 tablespoon olive oil

2 cloves garlic, minced

1 teaspoon dried dill

Salt and pepper to taste

Lemon cuts for decorating

Guidelines:

Preheat the broiler to 400°F (200°C).

Put every salmon filet on a piece of foil sufficiently enormous to crease over and seal.

Orchestrate asparagus around the salmon filets.

Shower olive oil over the salmon and asparagus.

Sprinkle minced garlic, dried dill, salt, and pepper equally over each filet and the asparagus.

Seal the foil bundles firmly.

Put the bundles on a baking sheet and heat for around 15-20 minutes or until the salmon is cooked through and the asparagus is delicate.

Cautiously open the foil parcels, decorate them with lemon cuts, and serve.

This recipe gives an equilibrium of protein, solid fats, and fiber-rich veggies. Change fixings and parts given individual necessities and inclinations.

# Chapter 6: Desserts and Sweets

## Sugar Substitutes

For diabetes patients, appropriate sugar substitutes incorporate stevia, erythritol, and protein-rich natural products.

other diabetes-accommodating sugar substitutes incorporate xylitol and sucralose. It's fundamental to consider glycemic record and individual resistance.

Normal sugar substitutes:

Stevia: Extricated from the leaves of the Stevia plant.

Erythritol: A sugar liquor tracked down in certain products of the soil food varieties.

Priest Natural product: Got from priest leafy foods seriously sweet.

Xylitol: A sugar liquor tracked down in many products of the soil.

Sucralose: An engineered sugar, frequently utilized in business sugar substitutes.

Continuously check item marks and counsel medical services proficiently for customized direction.

Here is a basic recipe for a diabetes-accommodating treat:

Sans sugar Berry Parfait:

Fixings:

1 cup blended berries (strawberries, blueberries, raspberries)

1 cup Greek yogurt (unsweetened)

1 teaspoon vanilla concentrate

1-2 tablespoons cleaved nuts (like almonds or pecans)

Guidelines:

In a bowl, blend Greek yogurt with vanilla concentrate.

Layer the lower part of serving glasses or bowls with a spoonful of the yogurt combination.

Add a layer of blended berries on top.

Rehash the layers until the glass is filled.

Top with slashed nuts for crunch and added flavor.

Chill in the cooler for something like 30 minutes before serving.

This treat isn't just delightful yet in addition diabetes-accommodating, offering regular pleasantness from berries without added sugars. Change segments in light of your dietary necessities.

Here is a flavorful and diabetes-accommodating recipe:

Barbecued Lemon Spice Chicken:

Fixings:

4 boneless, skinless chicken bosoms

2 tablespoons olive oil

2 cloves garlic, minced

1 teaspoon dried thyme

1 teaspoon dried rosemary

Zing and juice of 1 lemon

Salt and pepper to taste

Guidelines:

In a little bowl, blend olive oil, garlic, thyme, rosemary, lemon zing, lemon squeeze, salt, and pepper to make a marinade.

Place chicken bosoms in a resealable plastic pack or shallow dish, pour the marinade over them, and guarantee they are equitably covered. Marinate in the fridge for somewhere around 30 minutes.

Preheat the barbecue or barbecue skillet over medium-high intensity.

Barbecue the chicken for around 6-8 minutes for every side or until the inward temperature comes to 165°F (74°C) and the chicken is cooked through.

Let the chicken rest for a couple of moments before serving.

This barbecued chicken is tasty, low in starches, and an extraordinary choice for a diabetes-accommodating feast. Change flavors to suit your taste inclinations.

# Diabetic–Friendly Desserts

What about attempting a sans-sugar cheesecake with almond flour covering or a dim chocolate avocado mousse? These can be delightful choices for those searching for diabetic-accommodating pastries.

Consider making without-sugar berry popsicles utilizing normal sugars, similar to stevia or erythritol. Another choice is a cinnamon-flavored heated apple, which is both scrumptious and low in added sugars. Moreover, you could partake in a Greek yogurt parfait with new berries and a sprinkle of nuts for added surface.

What about trying different things with a chia seed pudding made with unsweetened almond milk and finished off with cut strawberries? On the other hand, you could prepare sans-sugar almond flour treats or attempt a without-sugar pumpkin pie with a nut covering for an occasional treat. These choices give pleasantness without spiking glucose levels.

You can likewise investigate a sans sugar coconut and lime sorbet for an invigorating pastry. Another thought is to make a crustless ricotta cheesecake improved with a sugar substitute. If you partake in a warm sweet, consider baking sans sugar-poached pears with a dash of cinnamon. These choices offer assortment while holding sugar content within proper limits.

What about making a without-sugar chocolate chia seed mousse or a no-sugar-added peanut butter protein balls? Furthermore, you can enjoy a sugar vanilla custard made with a sugar substitute like Priest natural product or stevia. These treats give fulfilling flavors without settling on your diabetic-accommodating necessities.

For a without-sugar chocolate chia seed mousse, you'll require:

2 tablespoons chia seeds

1 cup unsweetened almond milk

2 tablespoons unsweetened cocoa powder

1-2 tablespoons sugar substitute (like erythritol or stevia)

1/2 teaspoon vanilla concentrate

For no-sugar-added peanut butter protein balls:

1 cup normal peanut butter

1/2 cup protein powder (vanilla or chocolate enhanced)

2-3 tablespoons sugar substitute (erythritol or stevia)

1/4 cup almond flour

A spot of salt

For sans-sugar vanilla custard:

2 cups unsweetened almond milk

4 egg yolks

1/4 cup sugar substitute (priest natural product or stevia)

1 teaspoon vanilla concentrate

Go ahead and change the amounts in light of your taste inclinations. Partake in your diabetic-accommodating treats!

Here are the recipes for the sans-sugar chocolate chia seed mousse, no-sugar-added peanut butter protein balls, and without-sugar vanilla custard:

Sans sugar Chocolate Chia Seed Mousse:

In a bowl, blend chia seeds, unsweetened almond milk, cocoa powder, sugar substitute, and vanilla concentrate.

Whisk completely to guarantee even conveyance.

Cover the bowl and refrigerate for something like 3 hours or short-term.

Before serving, mix the blend well. Change pleasantness to taste.

Serve chilled and partake in your chocolate chia seed mousse!

No-Sugar-Added Peanut Butter Protein Balls:

In a blending bowl, consolidate peanut butter, protein powder, sugar substitute, almond flour, and a spot of salt.

Blend until all around joined. On the off chance that the combination is excessively dry, you can add somewhat more peanut butter.

Fold the blend into reduced-down balls and put them on a material-lined plate.

Refrigerate for somewhere around 30 minutes to solidify.

When set, store it in an impenetrable holder in the cooler.

Sans sugar Vanilla Custard:

In a pan, heat unsweetened almond milk until it's warm yet not bubbling.

In a different bowl, whisk together egg yolks and sugar substitute until very much joined.

Gradually empty the warm almond milk into the egg blend, whisking ceaselessly.

Empty the blend once more into the pot and cook over low intensity, mixing continually until it thickens.

Eliminate from heat, mix in vanilla concentrate, and let it cool.

Once cooled, refrigerate for a couple of hours until the custard sets.

Partake in these delectable and diabetic-accommodating pastries!

The following are two additional diabetic-accommodating sweet recipes for you:

Sans sugar Berry Popsicles:

Mix your #1 berries (strawberries, blueberries, raspberries) with a sugar substitute (like stevia or erythritol) until smooth.

Empty the blend into popsicle molds.

Embed popsicle sticks and freeze for something like 4 hours or until strong.

Run the molds under warm water to deliver the popsicles.

Invigorating and normally improved berry popsicles are prepared to appreciate!

Sans sugar Prepared Apple with Cinnamon:

Preheat your stove to 375°F (190°C).

Center and cut apples, leaving the skin on.

Place apple cuts in a baking dish and sprinkle with ground cinnamon.

Whenever wanted, add a sugar substitute to improve (discretionary).

Heat for around 20-25 minutes or until the apples are delicate.

Serve warm, and you have an encouraging, without-sugar-heated apple dessert.

Go ahead and change these recipes because of your inclinations and partake in these delicious, diabetic-accommodating treats!

# Chapter 7: Sample Meal Plans

## Daily Meal Plans

I can propose a few general thoughts for an everyday feast plan for people with diabetes.

Breakfast:

Entire grain oat with low-fat milk

A serving of berries

Fried eggs or egg whites

Early in the day Bite:

Greek yogurt with a small bunch of nuts

Crude vegetables with hummus

Lunch:

Barbecued chicken or fish

Quinoa or earthy-colored rice

Blended vegetables or a plate of mixed greens with various brilliant veggies

Evening Bite:

Apple cuts with peanut butter

Curds with pineapple

Supper:

Prepared or barbecued lean protein (chicken, turkey, tofu)

Steamed or broiled non-boring vegetables (broccoli, cauliflower)

Yam or entire-grain pasta

Evening Bite (if necessary):

A little small bunch of almonds or pecans

Sans sugar yogurt

Make sure to screen segment sizes, center around entire food varieties, and spread dinners over the day. Changes might be important in light of individual requirements and prescriptions. Continuously talk with a medical care professional for customized direction.

here are extra choices for a diabetes-accommodating dinner plan:

7. Breakfast Variety:

Oats made with water finished off with cut strawberries and a sprinkle of chia seeds

Hard-bubbled egg

8. Early in the day Nibble Variety:

Modest bunch of cherry tomatoes with mozzarella cheddar

A little orange or a piece of natural product

9. Lunch Variety:

Lentil or chickpea salad with tomatoes, cucumbers, and feta cheddar

The entire grain roll or wrap

10. Evening Nibble Variety:

Carrot and cucumber sticks with tzatziki

Little small bunch of sunflower seeds

11. Supper Variety:

Sautéed tofu with broccoli, ringer peppers, and snap peas

Quinoa or cauliflower rice

12. Evening Nibble Variety (if necessary):

Sans sugar gelatin

A couple of child carrots with hummus

Keep in mind that it's fundamental to screen glucose levels, remain hydrated, and tailor the arrangement to individual inclinations and nourishing requirements. Standard correspondence with medical services is vital for overseeing diabetes.

here are extra dinner thoughts for a diabetes-accommodating arrangement:

13. Breakfast Variety:

Entire grain toast with avocado

Smoked salmon or turkey cuts

Cut tomatoes and a sprinkle of spices

14. Early in the day Nibble Variety:

Curds with cut peaches

Entire grain wafers with cheddar

15. Lunch Variety:

Barbecued shrimp or tofu salad with blended greens

Cherry tomatoes, cucumber, and a vinaigrette dressing

Quinoa or grain

16. Evening Nibble Variety:

Modest bunch of edamame

A little apple with a piece of cheddar

17. Supper Variety:

Heated cod or salmon

Cooked Brussels fledglings and asparagus

Wild rice or couscous

18. Evening Nibble Variety (if necessary):

Sans sugar yogurt parfait with berries

Almond spread on entire grain wafers

These varieties give a blend of supplements, including fiber, lean proteins, and solid fats, which can help oversee glucose levels. Change segment sizes in light of individual requirements and inclinations. Continuously talk with a medical services professional for customized guidance.

here are extra feast thoughts for a diabetes-accommodating arrangement:

19. Breakfast Variety:

Smoothie with unsweetened almond milk, spinach, berries, and a scoop of protein powder

Entire grain English biscuit with a slim spread of almond margarine

20. Early in the day Nibble Variety:

Plain, non-fat Greek yogurt with a sprinkle of honey

Modest bunch of blended nuts (like almonds, pecans, and pistachios)

21. Lunch Variety:

Turkey or chicken lettuce wraps with destroyed carrots and cucumber

Quinoa salad with diced tomatoes, dark beans, and a lime vinaigrette

22. Evening Nibble Variety:

Cut pear with a little part of brie cheddar

Celery sticks with cream cheddar

23. Supper Variety:

Prepared chicken bosom with rosemary and lemon

Steamed broccoli and cauliflower

Bulgur or entire grain couscous

24. Evening Nibble Variety (if necessary):

Chia seed pudding made with almond milk

A little modest bunch of grapes

These choices keep on zeroing in on adjusted feasts, consolidating various supplement thick food varieties. Make sure to customize the arrangement because of individual dietary inclinations and talk with a medical care professional for custom-made guidance.

Here is a rundown of fixings that you can use to make various feasts for a diabetes-accommodating eating regimen:

Proteins:

Chicken bosom or turkey

Fish (salmon, cod, tilapia)

Tofu or tempeh

Lean meat or pork

Eggs

Low-fat curds

Greek yogurt (unsweetened, low-fat)

Vegetables:

8. Mixed greens (spinach, kale, arugula)

Broccoli

Cauliflower

Brussels sprouts

Chime peppers

Tomatoes

Cucumbers

Zucchini

Entire Grains:

16. Quinoa

Earthy colored rice

Grain

Bulgur

Entire grain pasta

Oats (steel-cut or rolled)

Vegetables:

22. Lentils

Chickpeas

Dark beans

Kidney beans

Natural products:

26. Berries (strawberries, blueberries, raspberries)

Apples

Pears

Oranges

Kiwi

Sound Fats:

31. Avocado

Nuts (almonds, pecans, pistachios)

Seeds (chia seeds, flaxseeds)

Olive oil

Dairy or Dairy Choices:

35. Low-fat milk

Unsweetened almond milk

Sauces and Flavorings:

37. Spices and flavors (rosemary, thyme, cumin, cinnamon)

Garlic

Ginger

Balsamic vinegar

Mustard (dijon or entire grain)

Make sure to pick low-sugar or without-sugar choices when appropriate, and be aware of part estimates. Tailor your feasts in light of individual inclinations and healthful prerequisites. Continuously talk with a medical services professional for customized counsel.

The following are two basic and diabetes-accommodating recipes for you:

1. Barbecued Lemon Spice Chicken with Cooked Vegetables

Fixings:

4 boneless, skinless chicken bosoms

2 lemons (squeezed)

2 tablespoons olive oil

2 cloves garlic (minced)

1 teaspoon dried oregano

1 teaspoon dried thyme

Salt and pepper to taste

Directions:

In a bowl, combine one lemon juice, olive oil, minced garlic, oregano, thyme, salt, and pepper.

Marinate chicken bosoms in the combination for somewhere around 30 minutes.

Preheat the barbecue. Barbecue chicken for around 6-8 minutes for each side or until completely cooked.

While the chicken is barbecuing, throw your number one vegetables (like zucchini, ringer peppers, and cherry tomatoes) with olive oil, salt, and pepper.

Broil the vegetables on the stove at 400°F (200°C) for 15-20 minutes or until they're delicate.

Serve the barbecued chicken over a bed of simmered vegetables.

2. Quinoa and Dark Bean Salad

Fixings:

1 cup quinoa (flushed)

2 cups water or vegetable stock

1 can (15 oz) dark beans (flushed and depleted)

1 cup cherry tomatoes (divided)

1 cucumber (diced)

1/4 cup red onion (finely slashed)

1/4 cup new cilantro (slashed)

2 tablespoons olive oil

2 tablespoons lime juice

Salt and pepper to taste

Directions:

In a pot, consolidate quinoa and water or vegetable stock. Heat to the point of boiling, then decrease intensity, cover, and stew for 15 minutes or until quinoa is cooked and water is consumed.

In a huge bowl, consolidate cooked quinoa, dark beans, cherry tomatoes, cucumber, red onion, and cilantro.

In a little bowl, whisk together olive oil, lime squeeze, salt, and pepper.

Pour the dressing over the quinoa blend and throw to consolidate.

Chill in the cooler for something like 30 minutes before serving.

These recipes give an equilibrium of protein, fiber, and sound fats. Change segment sizes in light of your dietary requirements and inclinations. Continuously talk with a medical care proficient for customized counsel.

# Weekly Meal Planning

For diabetes patients, center around offset feasts with lean proteins, entire grains, and a lot of vegetables. Plan dinners to incorporate different food sources to guarantee supplement admission. Consider counseling a dietitian for customized guidance.

Here is a basic week-by-week feast plan for diabetes patients:

Day 1:

Breakfast: Oats with berries and a sprinkle of chia seeds.

Lunch: Barbecued chicken plate of mixed greens with blended greens, cherry tomatoes, and vinaigrette.

Supper: Heated salmon, quinoa, and steamed broccoli.

Day 2:

Breakfast: Greek yogurt with cut almonds and a shower of honey.

Lunch: Turkey and avocado wrap with entire grain tortilla.

Supper: Sautéed tofu with bright ringer peppers and earthy-colored rice.

Day 3:

Breakfast: Fried eggs with spinach and entire grain toast.

Lunch: Lentil soup and a side of blended green plate of mixed greens.

Supper: Barbecued shrimp, yam, and asparagus.

Day 4:

Breakfast: Entire grain oat with low-fat milk and cut banana.

Lunch: Quinoa salad with chickpeas, cucumber, and feta cheddar.

Supper: Prepared chicken bosom, cooked Brussels sprouts, and quinoa.

Day 5:

Breakfast: Smoothie with spinach, berries, and plain Greek yogurt.

Lunch: Salmon and avocado sushi rolls with a side of miso soup.

Supper: Lean meat pan sear with broccoli and earthy-colored rice.

Day 6:

Breakfast: Curds with pineapple pieces and pecans.

Lunch: Entire grain pasta with pureed tomatoes, veggies, and barbecued chicken.

Supper: Heated cod, yam wedges, and green beans.

Day 7:

Breakfast: Peanut butter and banana entire grain toast.

Lunch: Chickpea and vegetable curry with quinoa.

Supper: Turkey meatballs, zucchini noodles, and marinara sauce.

Make sure to screen segment sizes, spread feasts over the day, and remain hydrated. Change given individual inclinations and counsel medical care proficient for customized direction.

Here is a rundown of elements for the week-after-week dinner plan:

Normal Fixings:

Lean proteins: Chicken bosom, salmon, tofu, turkey, shrimp, lean hamburger.

Entire grains: Cereal, quinoa, earthy colored rice, entire grain tortillas, entire grain bread, entire grain pasta.

Vegetables: Spinach, broccoli, ringer peppers, tomatoes, yams, asparagus, Brussels sprouts, cucumber.

Organic products: Berries (blueberries, strawberries), banana, pineapple.

Vegetables: Lentils, chickpeas.

Dairy or options: Greek yogurt, low-fat milk, curds.

Nuts and seeds: Almonds, chia seeds, pecans.

Sound fats: Avocado, olive oil.

Fixings: Vinaigrette, honey, miso glue, marinara sauce.

Flavors and spices: Use spices like basil, and thyme, and flavors like cumin, and paprika for some character.

Go ahead and alter the rundown in light of your inclinations and dietary requirements. Change amounts in light of the quantity of servings you intend to get ready.

Here are straightforward recipes for two or three of the dinners referenced:

Barbecued Chicken Plate of mixed greens:

Fixings:

Chicken bosom

Blended salad greens

Cherry tomatoes

Olive oil

Balsamic vinegar

Salt and pepper to taste

Directions:

Season chicken bosom with salt and pepper.

Barbecue the chicken until completely cooked.

In a bowl, blend salad greens and cherry tomatoes.

Cut barbecued chicken and put it on top of the plate of mixed greens.

Shower with olive oil and balsamic vinegar.

Veggie lover Quinoa Salad:

Fixings:

Quinoa

Chickpeas (canned or cooked)

Cucumber, diced

Feta cheddar disintegrated

Olive oil

Lemon juice

New mint leaves (discretionary)

Salt and pepper to taste

Guidelines:

Cook quinoa as indicated by bundle guidelines.

In a bowl, join cooked quinoa, chickpeas, diced cucumber, and disintegrated feta cheddar.

In a different bowl, whisk together olive oil, lemon squeeze, salt, and pepper.

Pour the dressing over the quinoa blend and throw to consolidate.

Embellish with new mint leaves whenever wanted.

Go ahead and adjust these recipes in light of your taste inclinations and dietary necessities.

The following are a couple more recipes:

Sautéed Tofu with Vegetables:

Fixings:

Firm tofu, cubed

Blended vegetables (ringer peppers, broccoli, carrots)

Soy sauce

Sesame oil

Garlic, minced

Ginger, ground

Green onions slashed

Sesame seeds for decorating

Guidelines:

Heat sesame oil in a skillet and sauté garlic and ginger until fragrant.

Add cubed tofu and sautéed food until delicately seared.

Add blended vegetables and sautéed food until delicate and fresh.

Pour soy sauce over the combination and throw until all around covered.

Decorate with cleaved green onions and sesame seeds.

Heated Cod with Lemon and Spices:

Fixings:

Cod filets

Lemon, cut

New spices (like dill or parsley), slashed

Olive oil

Garlic, minced

Salt and pepper to taste

Guidelines:

Preheat the broiler to 375°F (190°C).

Place cod filets in a baking dish.

Shower with olive oil and sprinkle minced garlic, salt, and pepper.

Top with lemon cuts and new spices.

Heat in the broiler for around 15-20 minutes or until the fish is cooked through.

Go ahead and change these recipes to suit your inclinations and dietary necessities. Partake in your flavorful and nutritious feasts!

# Chapter 8: Cooking Tips and Techniques

## Cooking for Diabetes

Cooking for diabetes includes zeroing in on offset feasts with controlled segments. Pick entire grains, lean proteins, and a lot of non-dull vegetables. Limit added sugars and settle on better cooking strategies like baking, barbecuing, or steaming. Customary checking of starch admission is vital for overseeing glucose levels.

Integrate fiber-rich food varieties, like beans and vegetables, to assist with glucose control. Pick sound fats like olive oil and avocados. Explore different avenues regarding spices and flavors to improve flavor without depending on unnecessary salt or sugar. Remain hydrated, and consider more modest, more successive dinners for the day to keep up with consistent glucose levels.

Preparing time can be useful. Incorporate various beautiful vegetables to guarantee a scope of supplements. Pick lean protein sources like poultry, fish, and tofu. Be aware of piece sizes, and hold back nothing adjusted plate. Ordinary actual work likewise assumes a key part in overseeing diabetes, so find exercises you appreciate and make them part of your daily schedule. Monitor your glucose levels to comprehend what various food varieties mean for you.

Consider integrating low-glycemic record food varieties, similar to yams and quinoa, into your dinners to assist with controlling glucose levels. Nibble on nuts or seeds for a solid, fulfilling choice. Limit handled food sources, as they frequently contain stowed-away sugars and undesirable fats. Checking glucose consistently permits you to make informed acclimations to your eating routine and way of life. Feel free to with an enlisted dietitian or medical services proficient for customized direction custom-made to your particular necessities and inclinations.

Remember these diabetes-accommodating elements for your dinners:

Entire grains: Quinoa, earthy colored rice, oats, and entire wheat give fiber and supplements.

Lean proteins: Chicken, turkey, fish, tofu, and vegetables offer protein without overabundance of fat.

Beautiful vegetables: Broccoli, spinach, chime peppers, carrots, and tomatoes give fundamental nutrients and minerals.

Sound fats: Avocado, olive oil, and nuts add heart-solid fats to your eating routine.

Low-fat dairy: Pick yogurt, milk, or cheddar with decreased fat substance for calcium and protein.

Vegetables: Beans, lentils, and chickpeas are great wellsprings of fiber and protein.

Spices and flavors: Use garlic, ginger, cinnamon, and different spices/flavors for flavor without added salt or sugar.

Berries: Blueberries, strawberries, and raspberries are rich in cell reinforcements and lower in sugar.

Here is a basic and diabetes-accommodating recipe for Barbecued Lemon Spice Chicken with Quinoa and Simmered Vegetables:

Barbecued Lemon Spice Chicken:

Fixings:

Chicken bosoms (boneless, skinless)

New lemon juice

Olive oil

Garlic (minced)

New spices (like rosemary, thyme, or oregano)

Salt and pepper to taste

Quinoa:

Fixings:

Quinoa

Low-sodium chicken or vegetable stock

Slashed parsley (for embellish)

Simmered Vegetables:

Fixings:

Grouped vegetables (chime peppers, zucchini, cherry tomatoes)

Olive oil

Garlic powder

Dried Italian spices

Salt and pepper to taste

Directions:

Marinate the Chicken:

In a bowl, blend lemon juice, olive oil, minced garlic, hacked spices, salt, and pepper.

Cover the chicken bosoms with the marinade and allow it to marinate for somewhere around 30 minutes.

Get ready for Quinoa:

Wash quinoa under chilly water.

Cook quinoa in low-sodium stock as per bundle directions.

Cushion with a fork, and trimming with cleaved parsley.

Broil Vegetables:

Preheat the stove to 400°F (200°C).

Throw hacked vegetables with olive oil, garlic powder, dried spices, salt, and pepper.

Broil on the stove until delicate and somewhat caramelized.

Barbecue Chicken:

Preheat the barbecue.

Barbecue the marinated chicken bosoms until completely cooked, with pleasant barbecue marks.

Serve:

Orchestrate barbecued chicken on a plate, close by a piece of quinoa and broiled vegetables.

This recipe furnishes an even dinner with lean protein, entire grains, and beautiful vegetables.

Change segments in light of individual dietary requirements, and partake in a delightful and diabetes-accommodating dish!

Here is a recipe for a delightful and diabetes-accommodating Spinach and Feta Stuffed Chicken Bosom:

Spinach and Feta Stuffed Chicken:

Fixings:

Chicken bosoms (boneless, skinless)

New spinach (cleaved)

Feta cheddar (disintegrated)

Garlic (minced)

Olive oil

Lemon zing

Salt and pepper to taste

Toothpicks

Guidelines:

Set up the Filling:

In a skillet, sauté hacked spinach and minced garlic in olive oil until withered.

Eliminate from heat, let it cool, and afterward blend in disintegrated feta cheddar and lemon zing. Season with salt and pepper.

Butterfly the Chicken:

Lay the chicken bosoms level and cut evenly, yet not the whole way through, making a pocket for the stuffing.

Stuff the Chicken:

Stuff every chicken bosom with the spinach and feta combination.

Secure with Toothpicks:

Use toothpicks to get the edges and keep the filling inside.

Cook the Chicken:

Preheat the stove to 375°F (190°C).

In a stove-safe container, singe the stuffed chicken on each side until brilliant brown.

Move the skillet to the preheated stove and prepare until the chicken is cooked through.

Serve:

Let the chicken rest for a couple of moments before eliminating the toothpicks.

Present with a side of steamed vegetables or a light plate of mixed greens.

This recipe gives a delectable blend of protein and vegetables while maintaining an emphasis on diabetes-accommodating fixings. Change the part measures as per your dietary requirements. Partake in your delightful and adjusted feast!

# Flavorful Seasonings without Added Sugars

For diabetes-accommodating flavoring, attempt spices like basil, oregano, and thyme, alongside flavors like cinnamon, cumin, and turmeric. These add flavor without added sugars, keeping a fair eating routine for diabetes on the board.

Consider utilizing garlic, onion powder, paprika, and dark pepper for flavorful dishes. Lemon juice, vinegar, and mustard are incredible for adding punch without added sugars. Explore different avenues regarding various mixes to upgrade the flavor of your dinners while keeping them diabetes-accommodating.

Select new spices like rosemary, cilantro, and parsley to hoist flavors. Integrate ginger and bean stew pieces for a smidgen of intensity. A blend of these flavors can make different and tasty choices for diabetes-cognizant cooking.

Investigate the rich warmth of flavors like nutmeg and cloves for an unpretentious pleasantness without added sugars. Moreover, utilize unsweetened concentrates like vanilla or almond to improve the flavor of treats without settling for less on diabetes.

Here is a rundown of diabetes-accommodating fixings:

Spices:

Basil

Oregano

Thyme

Rosemary

Cilantro

Parsley

Flavors:

Cinnamon

Cumin

Turmeric

Paprika

Dark pepper

Nutmeg

Cloves

Aromatics:

Garlic

Onion powder

Ginger

Citrus and Vinegar:

Lemon juice

Vinegar

Mustard:

Dijon or entire-grain mustard

Heat:

Bean stew pieces

Separates:

Vanilla concentrate

Almond separate

Solid Fats:

Olive oil

Avocado oil

Nuts and Seeds:

Almonds

Chia seeds

Flaxseeds

Proteins:

Lean meats

Fish

Keep in mind that consolidating different fixings can make delightful and diabetes-accommodating feasts. Continuously talk with a medical services professional for customized guidance.

Here are extra diabetes-accommodating fixings:

Salad Greens:

Spinach

Kale

Swiss chard

Non-Dull Vegetables:

Broccoli

Cauliflower

Zucchini

Ringer peppers

Berries:

Blueberries

Strawberries

Raspberries

Entire Grains:

Quinoa

Earthy colored rice

Oats (unsweetened)

Vegetables:

Chickpeas

Lentils

Dark beans

Dairy or Dairy Options:

Greek yogurt (unsweetened)

Almond milk (unsweetened)

Protein Sources:

Tofu

Skinless poultry

Greasy fish (salmon, mackerel)

Low-Glycemic Natural products:

Apples

Pears

Sugars (with some restraint):

Stevia

Priest natural product

Entire, Natural Food sources:

Eggs

Nuts (unsalted)

Seeds (sunflower, pumpkin)

These fixings offer a great many choices for making adjusted, nutritious, and tasty dinners reasonable for diabetes the board.

Here is a basic and diabetes-accommodating recipe for a Quinoa Salad:

Quinoa Salad with Veggies:

Fixings:

1 cup quinoa, washed

2 cups water

1 cup cherry tomatoes, split

1 cucumber, diced

1 chime pepper (any tone), diced

1/4 cup red onion, finely hacked

1/4 cup new parsley, slashed

2 tablespoons olive oil

2 tablespoons lemon juice

Salt and dark pepper to taste

Directions:

In a medium pot, consolidate quinoa and water. Heat to the point of boiling, then diminish intensity, cover, and stew for 15-20 minutes or until water is consumed and the quinoa is delicate. Allow it to cool.

In a huge bowl, join cooked quinoa, cherry tomatoes, cucumber, chime pepper, red onion, and new parsley.

In a little bowl, whisk together olive oil, lemon squeeze, salt, and dark pepper.

Pour the dressing over the quinoa blend and throw until everything is all around joined.

Chill in the fridge for no less than 30 minutes before permitting the flavors to merge.

This brilliant quinoa salad isn't just delectable but also loaded with supplements. Change the fixings as indicated by your taste inclinations, and go ahead and add barbecued chicken or chickpeas for additional protein. Appreciate!

Here is a diabetes-accommodating recipe for a Prepared Lemon Garlic Salmon:

Prepared Lemon Garlic Salmon:

Fixings:

4 salmon filets

2 tablespoons olive oil

2 cloves garlic, minced

1 teaspoon dried oregano

1 teaspoon dried thyme

1 teaspoon paprika

Zing of 1 lemon

Juice of 1 lemon


Salt and dark pepper to taste

New parsley for decorating

Guidelines:


Preheat the stove to 375°F (190°C). Line a baking sheet with material paper.

Put salmon filets on the pre-arranged baking sheet.


In a little bowl, blend olive oil, minced garlic, dried oregano, dried thyme, paprika, lemon zing, lemon squeeze, salt, and dark pepper to make a marinade.


Brush the marinade over the salmon filets, they are all around covered to guarantee they.

Prepare in the preheated stove for 12-15 minutes or until the salmon effectively pieces with a fork.

Embellish with new parsley before serving.

This tasty and sound-prepared salmon is rich in omega-3 unsaturated fats. Match it with a side of steamed vegetables or a verdant green plate of mixed greens for a total and diabetes-accommodating dinner. Appreciate!

# Chapter 9: Dining Out with Diabetes

## Making Healthy Choices at Restaurants

Pick barbecued or heated lean proteins like chicken or fish, choose veggies as sides, and request sauces as an afterthought to control segments. Keep away from seared and velvety dishes, and decide on entire grains whenever the situation allows. Focus on segment estimates, and think about sharing or taking extras. Continuously check sustenance data when accessible.

Choose plates of mixed greens with lean proteins, use vinaigrette dressings sparingly, and request entire grain choices for bread or pasta. Pick water or unsweetened refreshments rather than sweet beverages. Be mindful of toppings, as they can add stowed-away sugars. Ultimately, convey any dietary limitations or inclinations to the eatery staff for a custom-fitted feast.

Consider beginning with a stock-based soup or a serving of mixed greens to assist with controlling craving. Be aware of stowed-away sugars in apparently solid choices like smoothies or certain sauces. Barbecued vegetables can be a delightful and low-carb decision. If dubious about fixings or arrangement techniques, make sure to the server for additional subtleties.

Settle on high-fiber choices to assist with overseeing glucose levels. Pick prepared or simmered dishes over seared other options. Search for menu things marked "barbecued," "steamed," or "prepared." Be careful of liquor, and assuming you decide to drink, do so with some restraint. Prepare by looking at the menu online to make informed decisions before showing up at the eatery.

Consider integrating sound fats, like olive oil or avocado, into your dinner. Avoid the breadbasket or pick entire grain choices sparingly. Pick a new natural product or a little serving of a diabetic-accommodating treat on the off chance that you have a sweet tooth. Being aware of your decisions and piece sizes is vital, and make it a point for changes or replacements to more readily line up with your dietary requirements.

If conceivable, eat gradually to permit your body to perceive completion, assisting you with abstaining from indulging. Be careful of fixings like ketchup or grill sauce, as they might contain added sugars. Pick lean cuts of meat, and if there's a smorgasbord, study all choices before serving yourself to go with very educated decisions. In conclusion, remaining hydrated is critical, so hydrate all through the dinner.

Think about involving spices and flavors for flavor without added salt or sugar. Choose dishes that incorporate various beautiful vegetables for a scope of supplements. If you're dubious about specific menu things, feel free to your dietary necessities and request altered choices. Furthermore, keeping a food journal can assist you with following your dinners and distinguishing designs that function admirably for dealing with your diabetes.

Pick dishes that stress protein and fiber, assisting with balancing out glucose levels. Make sure to for replacements, for example, steamed vegetables rather than a side of fries. While requesting servings of mixed greens, be mindful of garnishes like bread garnishes and sweetened nuts that can add extra carbs and sugars. At last, be aware of part estimates, and consider sharing a course or bringing extras back home for another dinner.

Search for menu choices that focus on entire, natural food varieties. Consider bringing a little, compact glucose screen to assist you with settling on continuous choices in light of your levels. Hold back nothing of macronutrients, including sound fats, lean proteins, and complex starches. Furthermore, above all, partake you would say while pursuing decisions that help your general prosperity.

Pick eateries that offer dietary data, as it can direct your decisions all the more successfully. Pick barbecued or seared fish for a heart-solid wellspring of omega-3 unsaturated fats. If you're questionable about a dish's planning, make it a point to the cook or waiter for subtleties. What's more, consider having a little, adjusted nibble before eating to keep away from unnecessary yearning and indiscreet decisions.

While requesting refreshments, choose water, unsweetened tea, or dark espresso rather than sweet beverages. Be mindful of "diet" choices, as fake sugars might affect glucose levels for certain people. On the off chance that you're at a smorgasbord, begin with a little plate and fill it with different supplement thick choices. Lastly, centers around the social part of feasting as opposed to exclusively on the food, making the experience more agreeable and less fixated on dietary limitations.

# Managing Portions

For diabetes the executives, center around offset dinners with controlled segments. Incorporate fiber-rich food varieties, lean proteins, and solid fats. Screen starch admission, and consider more modest, more continuous feasts to assist with controlling glucose levels. Counsel medical services proficient or an enlisted dietitian for customized exhortation.

Pick entire grains over refined carbs, and be aware of the sugar content in food varieties. Settle on segment control instruments like more modest plates. Incorporate various bright vegetables for supplements. Routinely screen glucose levels to comprehend what various food varieties mean for you. Remain hydrated, and focus on standard, moderate activity. Individualized direction from a medical service proficient is significant for powerful diabetes executives.

Nibble cleverly on nuts, seeds, or low-fat dairy. Know about secret sugars in sauces and dressings. Figure out how to peruse food names to settle on informed decisions. Go for the gold dispersion of macronutrients in every feast. Keep a food journal to follow designs and recognize triggers. Keep in mind, that consistency is vital, and little way of life changes can prompt critical enhancements. Continuously counsel your medical services group for customized exhortations custom-made to your particular requirements.

# Chapter 10: Staying Active

## Exercise and Diabetes

Customary activity is advantageous for overseeing diabetes as it assists control of blood sugar levels, further develops insulin awareness, and advances general well-being. In any case, it's urgent to talk with a medical care professional to make a customized practice plan in light of individual necessities and well-being status.

Consolidating a blend of vigorous activities, strength preparation, and adaptability activities can be useful. Hold back nothing 150 minutes of moderate-force vigorous action each week, alongside strength preparing practices something like two times per week. Observing glucose levels when exercising is fundamental to comprehending how your body answers. Continuously stay hydrated and be aware of any side effects like wooziness or low glucose during and after exercises.

Furthermore, people with diabetes ought to consider factors like appropriate footwear to forestall foot confusion, customary eye check-ups, and acclimations to medicine or insulin portions because of workout schedules. It's fundamental to work out some kind of harmony between remaining dynamic and staying away from exorbitant strain, guaranteeing that work-out schedules line up with general diabetes the board objectives. Customary correspondence with medical services suppliers is key for adjusting the activity intended to change ailments.

While overseeing diabetes through work out, focusing on feast timing is critical. Eating a decent dinner or bite before practicing can assist with forestalling low glucose, while post-practice nourishment supports recuperation. Checking glucose patterns over the long run and changing the workout routine in like manner keeps up with stable glucose levels. Moreover, joining support gatherings or practicing with a pal can give inspiration and upgrade adherence to a solid way of life. Continuously focus on well-being and counsel medical care experts for customized exhortation.

# Incorporating Physical Activity into Your Routine

Remembering customary active work for your routine can help diabetes executives. Go for the gold 150 minutes of moderate-power practice each week, as lively strolling.

Pick exercises you appreciate to remain roused, like swimming, cycling, or moving. Strength preparing works, such as weightlifting, can likewise further develop insulin responsiveness. Screen glucose levels when exercising, and remain hydrated. Continuously talk with your medical services group before beginning another activity routine.

Coordinate short eruptions of movement into your day, such as using the stairwell or taking a speedy stroll after feasts to assist with controlling glucose levels. Consistency is critical, so track down a normal that accommodates your way of life. Change your movement level in light of how your body answers and counsels your medical services group for progressing direction.

Consider following your active work and glucose levels to distinguish designs. Blend high-impact practices with adaptability and equilibrium exercises for general well-being. Remember the significance of heating up and chilling off. Focus on a balanced way to deal with qualification for better diabetes the executives.

Investigate exercises like yoga or jujitsu, which work on actual well-being as well as advanced pressure decrease. Keep a solid load through a fair eating routine, supplemented by customary activity. Participate in exercises with an emotionally supportive network, making it more charming and simpler to remain steady. Consistently rethink and change your everyday practice depending on the situation with direction from your medical care group.

Integrate everyday exercises like planting or family tasks as extra types of actual work. Watch out for your footwear to forestall foot-related issues, particularly on the off chance that you have neuropathy. Be aware of your body's signs, and assuming you experience any surprising side effects during exercise, counsel your medical care supplier quickly. Consistently audit your diabetes the executives intend to guarantee it lines up with your developing requirements and generally speaking well-being objectives.

# Chapter 11: Monitoring and Managing Blood Sugar

## Importance of Regular Monitoring

Standard observing for diabetes is significant for overseeing blood glucose levels, forestalling confusion, and changing treatment plans. It assists people with pursuing an informed way of life decisions, identifying examples, and working intimately with medical care suppliers to guarantee viable diabetes executives. Observing additionally engages convenient meditation, lessening the gamble of difficulties like coronary illness, kidney issues, and nerve harm.

Predictable observing permits people with diabetes to figure out how their eating routine, exercise, and meds influence their glucose levels. This information empowers them to make essential acclimations to keep up with ideal glucose control. Normal checks additionally help in recognizing potential issues early, forestalling outrageous highs or lows that could prompt crises. Moreover, medical services experts depend on observing information to arrive at informed conclusions about therapy changes and give customized direction to better long-haul well-being results.

Besides, standard checking encourages a proactive way to deal with diabetes. It urges people to take part in their medical services, cultivating a feeling of control and strengthening effectively. By following patterns over the long haul, people can distinguish triggers, evaluate the viability of medications, and work cooperatively with medical services groups to streamline their diabetes care. This continuous cautiousness is fundamental for accomplishing and keeping a steady and solid way of life while living with diabetes.

Predictable observing oversees prompt worries as well as assumes a crucial part in forestalling difficulties that might arise after some time. It considers the early location of changes in glucose levels, which can add to diminishing the gamble of entanglements like vision issues, cardiovascular issues, and nerve harm. In addition, normal checking gives significant data to medical services suppliers to tailor therapy plans, guaranteeing they line up with a person's advancing well-being needs, eventually adding to long-haul prosperity for those with diabetes.

# Medication Management

Overseeing diabetes frequently includes a mix of prescriptions, way-of-life changes, and checking. Normal drugs incorporate insulin, metformin, and others custom-fitted to individual requirements. Meeting with medical services proficiently is vital for customized exhortation and changes because of glucose levels, way of life, and general well-being. Ordinary observing, smart dieting, and active work are necessary pieces of viable diabetes on the board.

It means a lot to accept prescriptions as recommended, stick to a fair eating routine with controlled starch consumption, and take part in normal activity to assist with overseeing glucose levels. Ordinary observing of blood glucose, alongside correspondence with medical care suppliers, empowers ideal acclimations to the therapy plan. Also, overseeing pressure and getting adequate rest add to in general prosperity of people with diabetes. Continuously talk with medical services experts for customized direction and acclimations to your diabetes the executives plan.

Laying out an everyday schedule is helpful for diabetes executives. This incorporates steady dinner times, customary active work, and prescription adherence. Checking glucose levels at assigned times, remaining hydrated, and integrating pressure-decreasing exercises into your routine can add to stable glucose levels. Redoing your routine in light of individual necessities and counseling medical services experts for direction guarantees a complete way to deal with diabetes care.

In your daily practice, focus on an even eating routine with accentuation on entire food sources like organic products, vegetables, lean proteins, and entire grains. Consistently check glucose levels and keep a log to follow designs. Guarantee legitimate capacity and organization of drugs, and feel free to any worries with your medical services group. Incorporate both high-impact and strength-preparing practices in your daily schedule, holding back nothing 150 minutes of moderate-power practice each week. Consistency in these practices cultivates better diabetes control and by and large well-being.

J

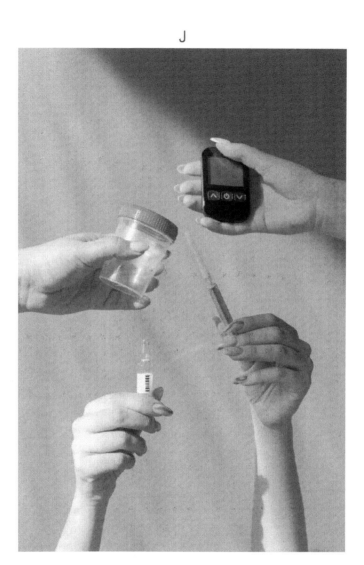

# Chapter 12: Frequently Asked Questions

## Common Concerns

Normal worries about diabetes incorporate overseeing glucose levels, potential entanglements like coronary illness or nerve harm, the requirement for a reasonable eating routine, and the significance of customary activity. Tending to these worries through appropriate clinical direction and way of life choices is urgent.

Individuals with diabetes frequently stress over the effect of weight on their condition, the requirement for reliable observation, and possible results of prescriptions. Moreover, there might be worries about the social and close-to-home parts of residing with diabetes, like shame or sensations of seclusion. Normal correspondence with medical care suppliers can assist with tending to these worries and offer fundamental help.

Weight the board is one more typical worry for people with diabetes, as keeping a solid weight can emphatically influence glucose control. A feeling of dread toward hypoglycemia (low glucose) and the monetary parts of overseeing diabetes, including the expense of meds and supplies, are likewise pervasive worries. Training and a complete way to deal with diabetes care can assist people with exploring these difficulties.

Worries about long-haul entanglements, for example, kidney illness, eye issues, and the possible effect on ripeness, are regularly on the personalities of those with diabetes. Furthermore, issues connected with movement, particularly while crossing time regions, and the requirement for predictable admittance to medical care can be causes of stress. Tending to these worries frequently includes proactive preparation, adherence to clinical exhortation, and progressing self-administration.

Mental viewpoints, similar to the apprehension about diabetes-related confusions or the pressure of everyday administration, are critical worries. The effect of diabetes on connections and relational peculiarities can likewise be tested. It's fundamental for people to focus on mental prosperity, looking for help from medical care experts, companions, or care groups to adapt to the close-to-home parts of residing with diabetes.

# Seeking Professional Guidance

I can give general data about diabetes, including the executive's methodologies and way of life tips.

Notwithstanding, for customized and proficient direction, it's vital to talk with a medical services professional, for example, a specialist or an enrolled dietitian, who can evaluate your particular well-being circumstance and give custom-made exhortation.

For overseeing diabetes, key viewpoints include:

Glucose Observing: Routinely check your glucose levels as exhorted by your medical care group.

Drug Adherence: Take endorsed meds reliably and adhere to your medical care supplier's guidelines.

Smart dieting: Spotlight on a reasonable eating regimen with proper piece sizes, underscoring organic products, vegetables, entire grains, lean proteins, and solid fats.

Actual work: Take part in normal activity, custom fitted to your wellness level and as endorsed by your medical services supplier, to assist with controlling glucose levels.

Weight The executives: Accomplish and keep a solid load to further develop insulin responsiveness.

Stress The executives: Practice pressure decrease procedures, as stress can affect glucose levels.

Customary Wellbeing Check-ups: Go to standard check-ups with your medical services group to screen your general well-being and address any worries.

Keep in mind, that individualized counsel is vital, so counsel your medical care proficient for direction well defined for your circumstance.

Here are a few extra ways to oversee diabetes:

Hydration: Remain very much hydrated by drinking a lot of water for the day.

Customary Rest: Guarantee satisfactory and quality rest, as it assumes a part in general well-being and can influence glucose levels.

Foot Care: Examine your feet consistently for any cuts, wounds, or indications of disease, and look for brief clinical considerations for any issues.

Stop Smoking: If you smoke, consider stopping, as smoking can add to diabetes-related confusion.

Liquor Control: Assuming you drink liquor, do so with some restraint, and know about its likely effect on glucose levels.

Instruct Yourself: More deeply study diabetes the board, as information enables you to come to informed conclusions about your well-being.

Emotionally supportive network: Fabricate areas of strength for a framework with companions, family, or a diabetes support gathering to share encounters and get everyday reassurance.

Keep in mind that these are common principles, and your medical care group can give customized guidance in light of your well-being status and requirements. Customary correspondence with them is significant for successful diabetes executives.

# Embracing a Healthy Lifestyle with Diabetes

Embracing a sound way of life with diabetes includes keeping a fair eating regimen, ordinary activity, observing glucose levels, and remaining informed about your condition. Talk with medical services experts to make a customized plan that suits your necessities and oversees diabetes successfully.

Notwithstanding dietary and exercise contemplations, overseeing pressure is vital for diabetes control. Normal check-ups, drug adherence, and keeping a solid weight add to general prosperity. Teach yourself about diabetes to the board, and consider support gatherings or directing for basic reassurance. Continuously counsel medical services suppliers for custom-made exhortation in light of your particular well-being needs.

Sufficient rest is fundamental for diabetes the board, as it impacts glucose levels and by and large well-being. Remain hydrated, limit liquor admission, and quit smoking if pertinent. Consistently screen your blood glucose levels, and be proactive in tending to any variances. Consistency in this way of life decisions encourages long-term well-being and forestalls difficulties related to diabetes.

Incorporate various supplement-rich food varieties into your eating routine, underscoring entire grains, lean proteins, organic products, and vegetables. Be aware of part sizes to manage calorie consumption. Consider including low-influence practices like strolling or swimming into your daily schedule, and go for the gold 150 minutes of moderate-power practice each week. Building areas of strength for a framework with loved ones can upgrade your capacity to explore the difficulties of living with diabetes.

Printed in Great Britain
by Amazon

35851203R00071